Making Short Film

Making Short Films On Your Smartphone

By

Michael Kaltenbrunner

Michael Kaltenbrunner

© Copyright 2015 by Content Arcade Publishing - All rights reserved.

This document is geared towards providing exact and reliable information in regards to the topic and issue covered. The publication is sold with the idea that the publisher is not required to render accounting, officially permitted, or otherwise, qualified services. If advice is necessary, legal or professional, a practiced individual in the profession should be ordered.

- From a Declaration of Principles which was accepted and approved equally by a Committee of the American Bar Association and a Committee of Publishers and Associations.

In no way is it legal to reproduce, duplicate, or transmit any part of this document in either electronic means or in printed format. Recording of this publication is strictly prohibited and any storage of this document is not allowed unless with written permission from the publisher. All rights reserved.

The information provided herein is stated to be truthful and consistent, in that any liability, in terms of inattention or otherwise, by any usage or abuse of any policies, processes, or directions contained within is the solitary and utter responsibility of the recipient reader. Under no circumstances will any legal responsibility or blame be held against the publisher for any reparation, damages, or monetary loss due to the information herein, either directly or indirectly.

Respective authors own all copyrights not held by the publisher.

The information herein is offered for informational purposes solely, and is universal as so. The presentation of the information is without contract or any type of guarantee assurance.

The trademarks that are used are without any consent, and the publication of the trademark is without permission or backing by the trademark owner. All trademarks and brands within this book are for clarifying purposes only and are the owned by the owners themselves, not affiliated with this document.

Table of Contents

INTRODUCTION 7
The Technology Side of Things 12
    Is Your Smartphone Good Enough? 12
    What Your Phone Should Have? 14
    Smartphone Camera Limitations 15
    Video Sensors 16
    So-So Lenses 17
    Other Effects 18
Smartphone Accessories 19
    Tripods 19
    Lenses 20
Mounts and Cases 26
    Remote Controls 26
    Audio 28
    Lights 30
    Extra Battery Power 31
    Additional Storage 33
    Extra Equipment 35
    Lighting 36
    Work Lights 36

- Household Lighting 37
- Portable Lighting 38
- Reflectors, Diffusers, and Filters 39
- Even More Equipment 41

Smartphone Film Making Apps Guide 43

Android Apps for Film Makers 44
- Camera Apps 44
- Google Camera 44
- Editing Apps 45
- iPhone Apps for Film Makers 47
- Editing Apps 48

Film Making 101 52
- Writing a Script 52
- Thinking of Ideas 53
- Titles 55
- Themes 55
- Length 56
- Climax and Rhythm 57
- Telling Your Story 58
- Characters 60
- No Script? No Problem! 61
- Getting it Done 62

Planning Your Shoot 62

Continuity 63

Smartphone Camera Work 64

Image Noise 65

Color Temperature 66

Frustrating Exposure 66

Framing 68

Shooting Indoors 69

Cast 69

Crew 71

Director 72

DOP (Director of Photography) 72

Sound/Lighting/Helper 73

Paying People 74

Editing 75

CONCLUSION 78

What Now? 78

INTRODUCTION

So, You Want to Make a Short Film?

You are reading this book because, like many others, you have a passion to create your own short film. There is a story inside of you, and it has been dying to come out. Maybe you already know what it is, or perhaps you'll need to find the right inspiration, in order to unleash that story. With the world of mobile technology putting quality video cameras in everyone's pocket, now is the best time to put your film making money where your mouth is. Do you want to make your very own short film, using your smartphone? Continue reading to learn just how to do so.

Why Do It?

Why would anyone want to make a short film on their smartphone? Surely a regular video camera would make things easier, right? Well, that's not the case these days. Technology changes the ways for each filmmaker to craft their art, and for the current generation — that involves mobile devices.

One of the biggest reasons for people to use smartphones, is the incredibly low cost of entry it involves. They're certainly not free, and can sometimes be quite expensive. But most people already have a smartphone, or know someone who will let them borrow. If you have a group of actors and crew members involved in planning a short film, there's a great chance that you have access to a whole pool of mobile devices already.

Because most people will have access to multiple devices, it's possible to set up some multi-camera shots, or even shoot in more than one location at a time. This is a long way from the days where you would have been lucky to get your hands on just one decent video camera.

As well as being relatively cheap, with some smartphones costing less than $100, they are also simple to use. With all of the great apps available on the popular apps stores, it's not difficult to find the right software for your needs. If you don't have any money for apps, you'll be glad to know that many of them are free. There's also the matter of "tape" or "film", neither of which is physically used much these days. With a device that can take SD cards for storage, it's possible to record an insane amount of footage. It can then be transferred to a harddrive or computer, or even synced online. Forget about spending loads of cash on your physical recording medium.

Apart from the costs and availability of the devices, smartphones give people the chance to film at any time, wherever they are. If you see something that would work brilliantly as part of your short film, you just need to whip out your phone and start filming.

If you are trying to stir up some buzz about a film that's in the works — deciding to shoot with a smartphone might get people's attention. It's true that it is still a relatively new, and somewhat "gimmicky" way to film things. At least, that's what some people will tell you. Because mobile devices are still pretty cutting-edge, you might be able to get some funding for a smartphone film, where a more traditional method of filming would get you no attention. That is certainly not to say that filming with smartphones is less valid. "Real" movies can be made with these devices, and you don't need to rely on them for the coolness factor alone.

What's In This Book?

Are you wondering just what you can learn from this book? To make a great short film, no matter what you use to shoot it — you need to learn the basics. The chapter called "Technology" will teach you more about what kind of smartphone you need, as well as add-ons and other equipment. If you don't have any money to buy things like lights and audio gear, you will love to information there. Next, you will learn about additional equipment that you might need, and how to improvise with everyday items.

"Smartphone Film Making Apps" will tell you which apps to get, so you don't need to waste your time trying dozens of them out.

The chapter called "Film Making 101" is there to explain all of the basics of film making. Once you're more familiar with that, you will be able to start practicing your skills. If you don't know how to make a good movie, no amount of money or equipment can help you. Once you've planned your film, you're going to need a cast to act in it, and some crew to help make it. This chapter also has everything that you need to know about that, as well as what to do with your video to edit it.

Michael Kaltenbrunner

The Technology Side of Things

Is Your Smartphone Good Enough?

A popular saying is, "The best camera is the one you have with you," and that's very true for this topic. As long as you have something to shoot with, you're all set. However, there are still some extra features and specs that will make things a lot easier.

As stated above, if you have something that can record film and audio, then yes, your smartphone is "good enough" to make movies. However, that does not necessarily mean that it's going to produce the highest quality footage in the world. Don't get too caught up in all the popular tech-terms, like "HD" and "megapixels". These things are often used by manufacturers to try and demonstrate that their products are somehow superior. Yes, the specs for electronic devices are important, but they can often be skewed, to make things seem better than they really are.

On the other hand, there are plenty of terrible films that were made with the best equipment money could buy. You don't need expensive equipment to make a great film, and all the money in the world certainly won't ensure that your work doesn't stink. Get the fundamentals right, and learn how to create something brilliant.

What Your Phone Should Have?

In order to make a short film with your smartphone, it does need a few basic features, as a minimum. Naturally, it will need a video camera, a microphone, and preferable an option for inserting additional storage, such as an SD or micro SD card. You don't need to have additional storage, but it's going to be pretty tough to shoot a film, especially if your phone only has a small about of space for footage. However, there are some great smartphones, such as the range of iPhones, that can't accept addition SD cards. These generally have 16GB, 32GB, or so of space. That is typically enough, depending on how much you plan to film. You might just need to transfer your video footage to a computer or other device, to make space throughout the shoot.

Smartphone Camera Limitations

It should be noted that there are some compromises to be made, when you choose to shoot with a smartphone. They are not dedicated video cameras, so it's important to understand what the differences are. So, how is a smartphone's camera different from a dedicated, high-quality video camera? They both have the same basic hardware for filming, including a lens, sensors, aperture, and appropriate software. They can also record at 720p, or even 1080p. Many smartphones can give you HD quality video. However, even with all of these similarities, there are some big differences.

When two different pieces of technology have the sames specs, you can be forgiven for thinking they will each produce identical footage.

Video Sensors

The biggest difference between and HD video camera, and an HD smartphone, is the image sensor. That's the part that takes the light, which reflects off whatever you're filming, and turns it into digital information. Most decent video cameras have sensors that are as big as 2/3 inch, measuring from each corner, diagonally. The better quality ones often have sensors that are larger than an inch. When you buy something as small and compact as a smartphone, there needs to be some compromises made with the size of the hardware. For example, the sensor in the iPhone 4 is just 0.31 inches. That's actually quite large, compared to many other smartphones.

Why is a bigger sensor better? The bigger they are, the more space there is for collecting light, and turning it into accurate looking images. In order to make a tiny sensor, which is still accurate, it must be extremely sensitive. The trade-off with this, is that it can produce more image "noise". That can give your pictures and video distortion, speckles of color, jarring, and a lower quality of color.

So-So Lenses

Another thing that will separate smartphone cameras from fully-sized video cameras, is the lens. When you use a camcorder or DSLR camera, you are typically shooting through a larger lens, and one with the ability to zoom. Compact camcorders, as well as smartphones, have smaller lenses. Their optics are also fixed, so you can't zoom. Yes, they do have zoom functions, but those are typically digital. If you "zoom" with a smartphone's camera, you are almost certainly just digitally cropping the image, and you will lose quality.

Fixed lenses on smaller cameras and smartphones aren't great at allowing light to reach the sensor properly either. That means you're going to end up with lower quality images. Don't worry, because you can buy a range of lens accessories, for many different types of smartphones. That will be covered later in the section.

Other Effects

Another peculiarity that you will notice with smartphone filming, is something called "rolling shutter". This basically leaves a rippled effect on your video, if you are shooting something that's moving quickly. This includes shots where the camera is being moved as well. Instead of scanning an entire frame at once, as with traditional cameras, a smartphone's sensor will scan from one side to the other. This effect can be avoided by using a tripod or mount. Of course, if you want to be creative, maybe a little rolling shutter could be incorporated into your footage on purpose.

Smartphone Accessories

Tripods

Unless you want all of your footage to be shaky (which is actually desired for certain styles of film), you will want to look into buying a tripod. Unlike regular cameras, with their universal mounting systems, smartphone film makers will need to get a special tripod or mount. Don't worry, because there are loads of them on the market. Finding the right one might be a little tough, since some tripods are poorly made. You wouldn't want to trust a cheap, flimsy tripod to safely hold your smartphone, would you? Take a look at some of the more popular smartphone tripods that are available at the moment.

Manfrotto makes a compact tripod, for use in the hand, or on tables and benches. It's called the Pixi, and stands at about 5.3 inches in height. The sturdy tripod legs can be folder together, to turn the gadget into a comfortable grip. You can use this tripod with regular cameras, but it will also attach to a smartphone mount. The legs are attached to a ball system, with a button, so that you can easily move them around, or lock everything in place. The *ManfrottoPixi* costs around $25.

Are you looking for something a little more flexible, literally? The JobyGorillaPod has been a popular design for several years. It grips onto your smartphone, and has flexible legs, which can be bent into many shapes. Do you want to be able to wrap your smartphone onto things like trees or benches? This is the perfect choice for you.

Lenses

Making Short Films on Your Smartphone

Apart from a few exceptions, your average smartphone camera has a lens with wide angel, fixed focal length. This basically gives you no options for zooming in and out, unless you physically move the smartphone. While that might work just fine for taking photographs at parties and at the park, etc., that's not going to cut it for many film makers.

It's great news that the market for smartphone lenses has grown rapidly in recent years. That's probably a result of the increasing quality of the cameras on phones, and more people taking the devices seriously, for "proper" camera work. You can buy different lens accessories, and kits with multiple options. It's a good idea to get a few, if you have the means, so that you can change them for different shots.

InstaLens are a great choice for people who don't have a popular model of smartphone, because they will work with many different devices. They are also a good choice for people with a small budget. You can choose from super-wide, wide-angle, fisheye, polarizer, and telephoto, but will need to buy each one separately. However, at about $40 each, you are not going to break the bank (even if you buy a few of them). They use a magnet system for mounting to your phone, with removable adhesive rings. That means you will need to stick them on, around the existing lens of your phone. If you want a full set, with all five lens types, it will cost you about $145.

Olloclip manufactures a range of popular, versatile, and reasonably priced options. They even have a four-in-one product, which works with Samsung Galaxy S4 or S5, and iPhone. This product can clip onto a phone, and can give you wide angle, fisheye, or macro options (for extreme close-ups). When you want to change your lens, it's just a matter of flipping them around, and then choosing the attachment that you want. These add-ons will cost you around $70 or so, which isn't too steep.

Moment Lenses make some of the finest optical gear that you are likely to find for a smartphone device. You can choose from telephoto or wide angle, and expect to experience superb image sharpness. They work with iPhone 4 and later, Samsung Note 3, Note 4, S4, S5, and Nexus 5. They come with a special plate for mounting to your phone. The iPhone 6 version comes with a custom case for mounting. Each type of lens will run you about $100, so the previous two lines of products are more affordable options.

It seems that smartphones have started to get larger, with people wanting bigger screens and longer-lasting batteries. They are still pretty slim, and ever-so-shiny. That's wonderful if you want to polish them up and have a device that looks sleek and sophisticated. However, it's not so great for trying to hold comfortably, when you're after a nice shot. To make sure none of your video footage is ruined by shaky hands or accidentally slips, a good mount or case should be considered.

There are plenty of different cases to choose from, and they start at as little as a buck. For shooting a film, you will want something that's nicely made, sturdy, and hopefully with some specialized features. For making your smartphone into a more suitable camera, choose something with good ergonomics, or possibly a special attachment, for extra add ons.

Manfrotto has iPhone cases that are available from a number of popular stores. They are made to allow people to use their smartphones like proper cameras. In addition to allowing you to get a better grip, they work with other MonfrottoKlyp add ons, such as their lights, tripod mounts, and lenses. At around $25, these are great choice for iPhone 6 and 6 plus owners.

Joby has a nice alternative for people who don't have iPhones. Their JobyGripTight has a spring-loaded system, so it will clamp securely around phones of different sizes. There are also three different model sizes, so you can get one for smaller phones, or even tablets. This mount often comes packaged with Joby's little tripod. However, it can also be used with most other smartphone tripods. Depending which size you want, the product costs around $15 to $30.

Mounts and Cases

Remote Controls

Sometimes you might need to position your camera in a confined space. That's one thing that smartphones are perfect for. However, a remote device might be necessary, to allow you to control your phone. These are useful for shooting wildlife as well, so that you can place your phone and then retreat to a distance. After all, you don't want to scare away the subject of your shot, do you?

The so-called "selfie stick" is designed to allow people to take photos of, well, themselves. They're typically extendable sticks with handles and attachments for holding cameras and smartphones. Of course, this book isn't about anything as silly as taking selfies (even though most people reading this are probably guilty of doing so). These selfie sticks are useful for getting some interesting shots. For example, you might want to place your phone up higher than you can reach, looking down over the shot. A selfie stick can act as a cheaper alternative to the cranes that are often used in big budget movies. You can also use them to give you a little more reach, for when you might want to have your camera looking out over a ledge, or around an awkward corner.

The XSories Me-Shot-Deluxe costs $50, but it's one of the best selfie sticks that you can buy. It comes with a remote control, and will work with most Android and Apple smartphones.

Would you rather just buy a separate remote? There are plenty out, but the MukuShuttr is a good choice. It costs around $40, and works with iPhones and lots of different Android phones. It gives you up to 30 feet to play with, in case you want to get as far away from your smartphone as possible.

Most stores that sell digital equipment, will stock generic versions of these items, so you can pick up something cheaper. After all, many people choose to make smartphone films due to having small budgets, so why spend big on brand-name accessories, that aren't necessities?

Audio

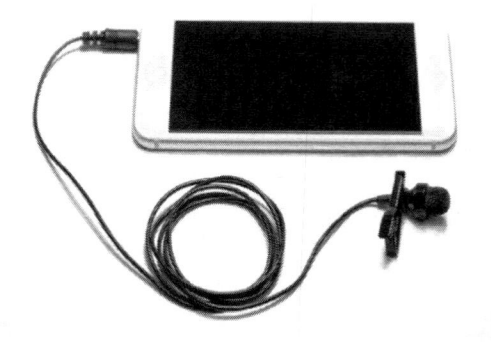

While many successful films have relatively low-quality video, people are less forgiving when it comes to sound. It's hard to cover up bad audio, so you really should consider using a good microphone device. Luckily, there are lots of options for smartphone users, and the prices aren't too steep.

If you have two smartphones to use, it's a good idea to record the audio on a separate device. A tablet, or audio recorder, can be used for this. Why would you want to split your sound and video up like that? It gives you the ability to have a dedicated sound person, who can deal with recording and monitoring your audio. They can plug a microphone into your second device, and put on some headphones to allow them to hear it during recording. This will give you loads of extra freedom. You can also have them get some secondary shots, giving you multiple angles to choose from — while the first smartphone can give you a second audio track to choose from (even though it won't sound as good with no microphone).

Lights

While you can buy special lights that attach to your smartphone, that's not always necessary. If you are filming in a location where you can set up some other equipment, it's always a better idea to do so. You should only worry about using lighting attachments, when you are "on-the-go", and can't set up proper lighting.

If you really want a light that attaches to your smartphone, which is better than the in-built LED, there are plenty of options to choose from. They range from compact LED devices, all the way up to professional-style lights, with remote controls and syncing functions.

The Pocket Spotlight from *Photojojo* is a nice choice, and it will only cost you around $30. It contains 32 LED lights, on a slim and attractive device. Instead of working like a flash, it will allow you to have a constant source of light. This can make setting up shots much easier, because you can see how it looks as you go. The device actually attaches to the headphone jack of a smartphone for power. In addition to that, you can get around one hour of lighting from the in-built battery, which charges through a regular USB port.

Extra Battery Power

One of the biggest dreads of any film maker, is running out of power at the worst possible moment. If you want to be able to keep shooting for many hours at a time — you should think about getting some extra battery power. Most smartphones have removable batteries, so this could be a good option. Of course, those extra batteries will only work with the one device. It can also be tricky to remove the panel on a smartphone, in order to insert a new battery — especially if you have mounts or accessories attached to it.

Why not save yourself the trouble, and use a portable battery charger? They are available from just about any store that sells mobile device accessories. They are basically just battery packs that you can plug USB devices into, to charge them. If you purchase a particularly high-storage battery, you should be set for at least one full day of shooting. The bonus here is that you can charge all of your USB devices, if you need to. If you're going to a remote location for some time, and you know you'll be away from power sockets — you might want to buy a solar powered charger.

Additional Storage

Many smartphones are able to take storage cards, such as SD and micro SD. In this case, you can simply buy a large card for filming. Make sure that you choose one that will actually work with your device, as some of them have size limits. These come in a range of sizes, from one GB, up to more than 100. If you think you will need more space than this, you have a few options. You could buy multiple storage cards, and then swap them as you need more space. This allows you to fit a lot of GBs in even the smallest pocket. The problem here, is that swapping those cards out might be a hassle.

You can actually plug USB devices into almost any smartphone, using a USB on-the-go adapter (also known as OTG). You should be able to buy one for just a couple of dollars, give or take. These plug into the data port of your smartphone, which is often also the power port. On the other end, you will find a regular USB plug. Android has been capable of using many different USB devices in this way, for quite some time. You will find that you can also use iPhone devices with some USB hardware. With this type of set up, you can simply use a USB stick, or even a portable harddrive. Once your phone's memory is full, simply transfer your footage onto a USB storage device, and you're ready to keep shooting.

USB storage devices are also a good idea to use for backup. You don't want to have something happen to your smartphone, that causes all of your carefully shot footage to get wiped. If you find that USB storage devices aren't compatible with your smartphone, you can either use an SD or micro SD card, or use a laptop to store your footage. Some portable harddrives work with Bluetooth or WiFi as well, so that you don't have to worry about plugging anything in. This allows you to wirelessly transfer your footage, from practically any device.

Extra Equipment

This book assumes that you don't have a huge budget, otherwise you might opt to buy an expensive video camera to shoot with. Even if you have zero dollars to spend on equipment, you can still get some wonderful footage. The real trick is how you set everything up, and also how creative you are.

Lighting

You have probably seen those big, fancy, expensive lights that professional film makers generally use. If you have a good budget, it's a good idea to get some for your shoot. For most people reading this book, cheaper is probably going to be better. You don't actually need to have "real" lights to make a great film.

Work Lights

Maybe you've seen these being used on construction sites at night. If you go to an auto or hardware store, you will likely find some of these for sale. Find some that come with a reasonably tall stand. Don't settle for the type that are on short stands, or you will have a lot of trouble setting them up for nice shots. You can find sets with two lights on one stand. Many of them have adjustable flaps on the sides or tops, to make it easier to direct the light. Buy whatever you can afford, but try to go for these extra features, if possible.

These types of lights have quite a lot of power, since they're designed to light up big areas at night. Of course, all of that power is going to be a little difficult to control. It's not likely that you will ever need to aim them directly on your actors or subjects. Instead, reflect them off walls or ceilings. Alternatively, you can use your own reflectors and diffusers, but that will be discussed later in this section.

The problem with powerful lights, is that they tend to get very hot. Be careful when you're moving them, or adjusting things. If you shop around, you should be able to pick up some great lights for as little as $10.

Household Lighting

The problem with video, is that it requires more lighting than the human eye. That means a regular light bulb, which is fine for homes, is not going to cut it for filming. What if you don't have any lights, but your shot is too dark? Try to find a lamp or two, and you can use them as makeshift film lights. Once again, you're going to need to get creative, in order to control where the light actually goes.

Portable Lighting

If you need to be away from wall outlets, try to find a decent flashlight or portable work light. They shouldn't cost too much, but you will need to buy enough batteries to last through all of your shooting. Portable spotlights are a good idea. The headlights of a car can work quite well, if you don't have anything else to use, or you need to light up a large area at night.

Reflectors, Diffusers, and Filters

These are used to allow you more control over your light sources. Before you can learn how to properly use them, you will need to get your hands on of your own. Luckily, they're easy to make, or improvise from household items.

Reflectors are used to bounce light onto things, like your actors. You'll be surprised to find how many things will do this, even though they're not shiny. A white sheet of card or paper can work well-enough, in a pinch. The reflectors that people place in their cars, to stop the dash and steering wheel from heating up under the sun, are perfect. They can also be folded up, making them highly portable. If you want something a little more solid, find a large piece of thick cardboard, and glue some tinfoil to one side. You can use the other side as well, if you need a very low amount of light to be reflected.

A diffuser is used to soften your lighting. They are placed on front of lights, and are often attached to the directional flaps on film lights. However, since you're not using professional gear, it's a good idea to keep them farther away from your lights. Otherwise, you will probably melt your diffusers, or even start a fire! Shower curtains work well as diffusers, but you can also use anything that's semi-opaque, like colored, plastic gift wrap.

Filters and "gels" are used to add different colors to lighting. If you've ever seen an old movie with a night scene in it, you might have noticed a blue tinge over everything. Blue filters are commonly used to allow enough light to fall on the shot, without letting things look too bright. You can use whatever colors you like, to make a shot that looks creative and unique.

Even More Equipment

Once you start to research the topic, you're going to find plenty of re-purposed equipment that you can make yourself, or find cheaply. These range from dollies made using skateboard wheels, to homemade camera cranes. Once you start to get into film making, you might want to try your hand at building some of these projects. However, for the purposes of this book, all of those things are a little too advanced.

There are some extra items that you might want to purchase, including extension cords for your power supplies, power strips, gaffer tape, a circuit tester, or even high-visibility vests for shooting near roads, and at night.

Before you head out to shoot, think about what you might need. It always helps to be prepared. One of the best parts about smartphone film making, is that you can often stay light. You don't really need much more than your phone, and maybe a few little accessories. What else you take is up to you!

Smartphone Film Making Apps Guide

One of the best parts about using a smartphone to make your film, is that you have a huge range of apps to choose from. The most popular devices in the world use either Android or iOS, so these will be covered in this book. The aim of this book is to show you how to do everything with your smartphone, from shooting, to editing, to sharing your masterpiece with the world. To make all of these things possible — you're going to need a few good apps.

Michael Kaltenbrunner

Android Apps for Film Makers

Camera Apps

When it comes to shooting video with an Android device, there aren't many options. A lot of the apps that you will find, are directed at people who want to put effects and filters on their photos. For this reason, Google's own camera app, or even most apps that come installed on smartphones, will be the best option.

Google Camera

Even though this is the stock app for some Android smartphones, it's still a good choice. The layout is easy to use, and there are some handy shooting modes available. You can touch the screen to focus on certain parts of your shot, giving you some manual control. There is also a timer function, an option for HD recording, panorama, lens blur, and of course the essential video recording function. The grid overlay option is also great, since it will make composing your shots a whole lot easier.

Editing Apps

KineMaster

This is really one of the best Android apps for professional video editing. If you want to have a range of great features, that are close to what you could find on a computer — there are few competitors. This might be a little too complex for people who just want to do some basic cutting or titles.

Some examples of what KineMaster can do include fading audio, using a range of different themes from the in-built library, and changing a whole host of settings for your video. The different icons will give you easy access to features, but you'll want to learn what each one does.

The free version of this software only allows you to export with a watermark over your video. If that's not desirable, you will need to pay for the full version. It costs $4.99 for a month's subscription, which should be enough time for many people to edit their film. If you'd rather have the app on a longer basis, it's $39.99 for a full year.

VidTrim

If you don't want to fork out the cash to get the full version of KineMaster, or you just don't need all those extra features, this is a great option. It lets you do small tweaks yourself, and there are also some pre-set options that you can choose from. You can do things like making your video black and white, or change the look of your footage. Of course, it allows you to trim your videos. It's not ideal for people who want to do any heavy editing, but the free version has full functionality, with advertisements. For just $2.49, you can remove the ads.

iPhone Apps for Film Makers

Camera Apps

The built-in camera app that comes with iPhones is a good choice. However, if you're looking for some extra features, you have a few good apps to choose from.

Video Camera+

This will only cost you $1 on the App Store. It gives you features like touch-to-focus, auto focus, and exposure settings. You can choose the video quality that you like, depending on what model of iPhone you have. The app can tag your videos with a location, to make it easier to sort through them during editing. The app allows you to turn the flash on as a continuous light, in case you don't have any other light sources to use. It also allows you to use a grid overlay, to make composition easier.

8mm Vintage Camera

Are you pining for that old-school look of real film? This app only costs $2, and it can do the job pretty well. While it doesn't have an option for shooting regular-looking video, it does have lots of great features.

Editing Apps

Pinnacle Studio

If you are looking for something with a decent range of professional features, look no farther than Pinnacle Studio. This app is aimed at people who want to do more than just trim down home movies. It's been around for a long time on desktops, and will give you all the control over the editing process that you're likely to need. The app will cost over $10, but that's a pretty nice price to pay for a full-featured video editing suite.

iMovie

This software has been around on Apple computers for quite a long time. It makes it simple to cut up your footage, and splice different parts together. These features alone will be enough for many people. It works on iPhones, iPads, and iPod Touch devices. If you want to be able to place titles, voiceovers, and music in your film — this is the best place to start. Since it only costs a few dollars, iMovie is a perfectly fine choice for smartphone movie makers.

Sharing Your Video

Once you have finished making your film, it's time to share it with the world. After all, most people reading this book want to make their own short film, so that other people can enjoy it. If you would rather hold onto your film, you can choose to create your own blog or website. From there, you can publish the films you create, so that people must visit your site to view them. If you'd like to go the more traditional route, you can export your film to a suitable format, and then treat it like any other video. You don't have to share your creations online, if you'd prefer to keep it between you, and your friends or family.

You have lots of options when it comes to video sharing services. Many of them are tailored to specific uses, like uploading short videos for friends to view. However, if you are going to share a complete short film, it's best to go with following options.

YouTube

YouTube really is the number one app for sharing video. Many people have become successful, after sharing their videos on YouTube. The service isn't restricted to short films either. People share home movies, music, live footage, documentaries, video game play footage, and anything else you can think of. It's the biggest video sharing service in the world right now. The mobile app is easy to use, and allows you to create your own channel, where you can share all of the films that you make.

The service works like a mix between a network of video channels, and a social media service. People can comment on your videos, provided that you allow it, and share them through other platforms. If you have something that becomes quite popular, you can make some money through advertising or subscriptions too.

Unless you want an all-in-one app for shooting basic videos, doing some very basic editing, and then sharing — YouTube is the app to choose.

Michael Kaltenbrunner

Film Making 101

While this book is about making a short film with a smartphone, it involves more than just technology. You can find out how to make films from a massive range of sources. There are books, websites, seminars, and university courses on the subject. There are lots of different opinions about the best ways to make a great film. Often, a film is loved by some people, and hated by others. This is an art form, so you need to make something that's special to you. No matter what you do, some people are going to dislike your film. However, if you want to make something that should be liked by a large number of people, you should start by learning the time-tested basics. This chapter will take you through the easy-to-understand film making basics.

Writing a Script

If you don't think you have good enough writing skills, find someone else who is willing to help out. While you might be able to come up with a great idea, someone is going to need to actually write the script.

Thinking of Ideas

Your film will need to start as an idea, before you can flesh it out into a proper script. It's hard to think of original ideas, because just about everything has already been done, in one form or another. Your goal should be trying to avoid cliches and trends, so that you can make something more original. Even if you come up with something that's been done before, try to find a new way to look at it. You might view the story from a unique perspective, or use some edgy filming or editing techniques. The world is full of stories and inspiration, so just look around and see what you can find.

Something funny or odd might have happened to you, or a person who you know. Maybe you've seen something in the media, and would like to make a statement about it. However you get your idea, you need to start by brainstorming. Just write down anything that comes to you, and don't hold back. This is not the time to worry about perfection, so just let the creative juices flow.

Next, you should start to focus on the idea that jump out at you. Choose whatever you like the most, and start to work them into an outline. Don't worry too much about how you're going to film things yet. Just try to work your best ideas into a cohesive outline. You can draw a line on a piece of paper, with the beginning on the left, and the end to the right. The middle will, of course, be your middle.

Titles

If you can think of a title for your film, it's going to be useful for writing the script. You can always change the title later, but avoid referring to it as just "the movie". Once again, brainstorm some idea. Think of titles that are catchy and interesting, but also give people an idea what the film will be about.

Themes

While films tell stories, they also share ideas and beliefs with an audience. These things comprise your theme, and it's an important part of good story telling. What ideas would you like people to take away from your film? Are there any things that you would like your characters to learn?

Length

Short films range in length from mere seconds, up to around half an hour. Around 3 to 10 minutes is a pretty good aim for your first film. There are no rules here, so feel free to do as you please. Since you don't have much time to tell your story, it's important to work out the most important things to tell the audience. You can't spend two minutes showing how your main character likes to make their coffee in the morning. And you also can't waste time with idle chit-chat between characters. Get to the point quickly, and keep people interested from the start, through the middle, and finally to the end.

Remember that making a short film isn't the same as a feature film. They have a lot of similarities, but are quite different in how you should approach making them. In a short film, you're only going to have around 20 minutes or less, to tell your story. There won't be room for dozens of scenes, or too many locations and characters. It's best to think of something that you can do on a smaller scale. That's why short film are great for people who have low budgets, or those who are just starting out with film making.

Climax and Rhythm

Think of your story as a roller coaster. You will start by coasting along in many cases, getting ready for things to start happening. You can choose to quickly raise the stakes, and have something exciting happen. As with a good roller coaster, you must have high points of excitement, followed by breaks in the tension. After something suspenseful, funny, or interesting happens, give the audience a break. Let them coast along again, or enjoy some minor bumps. Around the middle, you will want to have a large "bump", where things drastically change, or all seems lost. Next, you can work up to the finale. The final peak should come near the end, when everything is the most exciting or interesting. After that, you will have your final section, where things can be "summed up", before the ride is over.

Telling Your Story

Even the biggest budget, best actors, and fanciest special effects, can't save a truly terrible story. You should try to write a story that you can actually film. If you only have access to child or teenage actors, write a script that's about people from those age groups. If you are doing this by yourself, with just a handful of people, you're not going to be able to shoot an epic car chase.

Always think about what an audience will enjoy, instead of doing what's fun (unless you're just doing this for your own personal enjoyment). Make things visual too, since this is a film. Avoid having lots of dialog, where there isn't much happening on screen. The chances are that you will not have great actors who can make plain scenes exciting. Try to show what's happening in the story, by using pictures as a means to tell your story.

As a general rule, your story should have a main character with a goal. They should want or need something. Now, you need to think of obstacles that will stand in their way. These might come in the form of a person who's trying to stop them, or it could be a problem with society, or even nature. This works well if the "hero" is torn between wanting two opposing things, like doing the right thing, versus getting what they want for themselves.

A good story needs conflict and drama. If everything goes well, your audience will become bored. People like to see someone struggling, to a degree, and striving to try and make something happen. There must be things at stake, but your character should be willing to make an effort.

These are just some basic rules for making an interesting story. How you choose to make your script, is completely up to you. Maybe you would like to make a film that's about someone walking down the street, where nothing really happens. It's not going to interest most people, but you can make whatever pleases you. Perhaps you can use some very interesting camera shots, or odd lighting effects, which might draw people's attention.

When watching short films, people don't mind if you leave out a lot of details. They understand that there might only be a few minutes to tell a whole story, and will be happy to "fill in the gaps" themselves.

Characters

Your film will probably have actors in it, and they will be portraying characters. In a full-length film, there will be plenty of time to introduce your character, and allow people to get to know them. In a short film, you want to be a lot more economical with what you include. Think about a small handful of things that define your characters the best. Maybe they are overly nervous, or they lost their eyesight in a car accident. It's a lot easier to show only a few details in a short time, but you can really tell a lot with a few things.

No Script? No Problem!

So, you've decided that writing a script sounds too much like hard work? That's okay, because you can always improvise. Shooting with a smartphone means that you can take out your camera, no matter where you are, and let inspiration take over. The finished product might not be typical, as far as popular films go. Heck, it might not even make much sense. The most important part is that you enjoy what you're doing, and that you learn from the process.

Getting it Done

Now it's time to actually shoot your footage. This can be a stressful time for new film makers, so don't worry if things don't go according to plan. Having said that — the best way to ensure that everything goes smoothly, is to have a plan, and stick to it as much as possible.

Planning Your Shoot

Since you can edit your footage together later, you don't need to shoot everything in the order that it happens in your story. You might have several shots throughout your film that happen in one location, but are shown at different points. It makes sense to film all of those shots at once, while you're at the right place. You will want to make a plan, so that you know when you're filming which bits, and where. Write up a schedule for each day of shooting, and only ask people to come along if they're needed for that day.

Continuity

Have you even been watching a film, and noticed that someone's hair is suddenly parted on the opposite side, or they're wearing a blue shirt, when it was white just a second earlier? Continuity is all about avoiding these little hiccups, so that the audience feels like they're watching things happen in real-time. Of course, you will likely be filming different parts at different times, different places, or various days of the week. This is where it helps to take photos of your actors, props, and sets. Name the files so that you know when they were taken, and for which scene. Before you start filming next time, you can look at those photos, and make sure everything looks the same as it did during the last shoot.

Smartphone Camera Work

A smartphone will act differently to a regular camcorder or DSLR. If you are going to shoot anything "freehand", without a tripod or mount, be careful how you do so. Use both of your hands to hold the smartphone, and maintain a tight grip. Anything looser will give you some terribly shaky results. When you do move with the camera, go slowly. Don't use your arms or wrists to turn and position the camera during shots. Instead, try to use your whole body, twisting and changing heights as needed.

Even with a good camera, a fast movement will not work too well. If you're holding the camera in your hands, and it's a smartphone — the results are going to be pretty dismal with fast jerky movements. To get a more stable result, always hold your smartphone horizontally, as you would with a regular camera. This will not only give you a better grip, but it will make sure that your footage does not have black bars on the top and bottom.

Image Noise

You can fix this type of things later, during editing. However, the best approach is to avoid noise during filming. Try to get even lighting in your shots, so there aren't any areas with extreme shadows. If you want lots of contrast in the lighting of a shot, you might have to put up with some noise.

Color Temperature

You have to remember that different sources of light have their own color. The sun, for example, is actually a more blue color tone than many electric light bulbs. If you have multiple light sources in one shot, and they are different color temperatures, it can make things look the wrong color. Without proper white balance functions to fix this, you will need to be careful about placing multiple light sources in a shot. This way, your smartphone's automated color balance will not become "confused".

Frustrating Exposure

If you notice light in your shot that's bright white, you most likely have a problem with overexposure. Remember that smartphone camera sensors are highly sensitive to light, and they don't react well to lots of direct, bright lighting.

This can happen when you're outside on a sunny day, and it can make a blue sky look white. In order to solve this situation, try to shoot when there is more cloud coverage. If you are indoors, try not to point the smartphone directly at any lights, or you will get the same effect.

A cheap camera lens, paired with a sub-par sensor, will make it pretty tough to get good exposure in your shots. This will be more apparent for people using cheaper smartphones. But the problem will still be present, even with the higher end smartphones. As mentioned, you won't have all the manual features that come with DSLR cameras and expensive camcorders. That just means that you'll need to learn to control what's around you, instead of what's inside your smartphone.

Going out of the shade, when the sun's shining brightly, is going to result in some bad exposure. It's best to stay in the shade, and shoot bright scenes from there. Alternatively, you should wait for the sun to take a rest behind some clouds. As stated, the relatively small and cheap sensor in a smartphone will not handle highly contrasting light very well. If you really can't avoid being out in the sun's glaring light, try to get higher up to lessen overexposure. This way, you can place less of the sky in your shot, and give your phone's camera a change to even the exposure out.

Framing

Since smartphones typically lack manual adjustments for depth of field, white balance, and even focusing, you're going to need to be careful about framing. Try to position your subjects so that the aforementioned issues don't affect your shot. Rather than working with manual settings, you should learn how to work with automated features, to get the best results.

Shooting Indoors

You can have more control over what's happening in your shots, if you shoot inside. However, there are some different problems that come along with doing so. Try to avoid having any light sources behind your subject, or right in front of them. If you are getting bad exposure from light bulbs, use something to block the light. A semi-opaque piece of material often works, as long as it's not visible in the shot. Bouncing lights off walls or ceilings is a great way to diffuse light. When you are shooting with artificial light sources, avoid letting the sun come in through windows or open doors. As mentioned above, having multiple sources of light, with varying color temperatures, is a big "no".

Cast

When you are just getting started, you will probably ask friends and family members to act in your short films. This can work well in many cases. However, you will eventually get to a point where you want some more experienced actors. No one expects you to be able to call in Hollywood's A-listers, for your five minute short. However, you do have a lot of options available to you, no matter if you can actually pay your actors or not.

Start by contacting acting groups, universities, and even schools. You can also try putting advertisements on social media, or on classified websites like Craigslist. There are a lot of budding actors out there, and many of them would love the experience of being in a short film. Get out the word, and organize for people to audition for you. It will help if you can provide them with some excerpts of your script in advance, so they can prepare themselves.

Crew

Once you have your film planned, and the cast to act in it, you are also going to need people to help with the filming. If you plan to keep things minimal, you can shoot and direct everything yourself. This isn't ideal, but it is common for smartphone film makers to do most things themselves. If you can get some extra help, below are the basic roles that you should try to fill.

Director

You're going to need someone who understands the script, who can direct actors, and basically keep everything in check on the set. Since this is your film, it's likely that you will fill this role yourself.

DOP (Director of Photography)

This is kind of a fancy word for cameraman. However, a DOP is often in charge of composing shots, dealing with camera rigs and equipment, and actually shooting the video footage. Once again, you will probably want to do this job yourself. Often, one person is the director and DOP at the same time. There is nothing wrong with that either.

Sound/Lighting/Helper

Since this is a guide to smartphone film making, you're probably not going to have a huge crew hanging around and helping. You should find at least one person who knows their way around technology, and can be trusted to be helpful to you. They can assist with setting up lighting equipment, and holding a microphone in the right places (if you're not using the in-built microphone on your smartphone). This role can also include running back and forth between different people to convey information, gathering supplies, driving to the store for lunch, unpacking and packing gear, and any number of things. You will probably want at least one or two people to help out with these roles.

Paying People

While your friends and relatives might act, or help out as crew members, for free — it's a good idea to at least try to pay people. You might not have much money, but offering people $10 for a day of helping is better than nothing. If you don't have the cash, consider bringing along some lunch and beverages for everyone. Paying for transportation costs is another great idea. People might be willing to work for free, but it certainly shouldn't end up costing them money to help you out.

Editing

Once you have your footage, it's time to edit everything into a coherent film. You're going to have a lot of footage, most likely, so refer back to your online, script, and shooting schedules for guidance. Take your video files, and organize them in a way that makes it easy for you to edit. Place all the parts of each scene together in a folder, so they're easy to look at. Where you have multiple takes of the same shot, number them, or somehow label them.

Think of editing as cutting up your film, and then pasting together all of the bits that you'd like to use. Essentially, this is what you are doing, only with digital film, on your smartphone. Make sure that you keep a copy of your original footage, before you edit it. This will be useful, in case you decide to start again, or make changes later.

You can use audio from one take, and paste it over the video from another take. This might not work well for scenes where people can be seen talking, unless their lips sync up with the voice properly. You can also add sounds, like rain, the wind, or heavy traffic, over your sections of your video. In the same way, you can place music over your video, but make sure you have permission to use any songs you choose.

With editing, there are literally infinite options. You need to use the shots that help to best tell your story. You can use editing techniques to put many different spins on your footage, and create different rhythms and levels of tension. Once you get started, you will get a feeling for how you want to edit your film. The best thing about digital video as a format, is that it's easy to try different things. If you make a mistake, or create something you don't like, just go back to your raw footage, and try again.

Once you're happy with your editing, place the title text near the start of your film. At the end, you'll want to put some credits, with the names of your cast and crew, as well as anyone else who helped out with the film. And you have just created a short film — it's time to invite everyone around to view it, and cook up some popcorn!

CONCLUSION

What Now?

Once you've read the information in this book, it's time to put things into action. Maybe you've already started planning your story, writing your script, or actually shot some footage. Remember that film making is a form of art, and there are limitless possibilities. You can never truly master it, so there's always room for improvement.

The wonders of technology, like smartphones, have made film making accessible to more people than ever before. Try to use that to make new things, that were not possible in the past. Creativity and ingenuity are your best friends here, but dedication is also crucial. No one can tell you how to make the best short film, so get out there — and give it all that you have!

Printed in Great Britain
by Amazon